DISCOVERING THE WONDERS OF EUROPE'S WILDLIFE
A FUN-FILLED ADVENTURE FOR KIDS!

I0696399

ISBN: 9798391609100

European animals are wonderful due to their adaptability, diversity, ecological importance, and cultural significance. They have evolved unique traits to survive in harsh environments and play a vital role in maintaining ecosystems. They are also culturally significant, inspiring countless works of art and literature. Overall, they remind us of the beauty and importance of the natural world

CONTENTS

CONTENTS

STORY 1
THE GREAT DAM BUILDER: BENNY THE BEAVER SAVES THE BROOK

Once upon a time, in a dense forest near a babbling brook, there lived a beaver named Benny. Benny was no ordinary beaver. He was a beaver with a remarkable talent for building dams.

As a young beaver, Benny had always loved the sound of the water rushing through the brook, and he was fascinated by the way the water flowed. He spent hours watching the water and studying its movement.

One day, Benny had an idea. He thought that if he could build a dam, he could control the flow of the water and make the brook deeper and wider. This would give him and his beaver family more space to

swim and play.

So, Benny set to work. He gathered sticks, branches, and mud, and he began building his dam. It was slow work at first, but Benny was determined, and he kept at it day after day.

Soon, other beavers in the forest started to notice Benny's work. They were impressed by his determination and his skill. They had never seen a beaver build a dam like Benny was building, and they wondered if he would ever finish.

But Benny did finish. After months of hard work, his dam was complete. The water in the brook had backed up, and a deep pond had formed. The beavers could now swim and play in the pond, and they had more space than ever before.

But Benny was not content to stop there. He continued to work on his dam, refining it and improving it. He added more branches and sticks, and he carefully packed the mud to make it stronger. He even dug a channel through the dam to let some of the water flow out, so the pond would not overflow.

As time went on, Benny's dam became the envy of the entire forest. Other beavers would come from far and wide to see it and admire it. They called it the Great Dam, and Benny was hailed as the greatest beaver of them all.

But Benny was not satisfied. He knew that there was always room for improvement, and he continued to work on his dam day after day. He was never happy with it, and he always saw ways that it could be better.

One day, as Benny was working on his dam, he noticed something strange. The water in the brook was not flowing as it usually did. It was slow and sluggish, and it was starting to smell bad.

Benny knew that something was wrong. He swam downstream and found that a group of humans had built a dam on the other side of the forest. This dam was stopping the water from flowing through the brook, and it was causing the water to back up.

Benny knew that he had to do something to help. He called a meeting of all the beavers in the forest and explained the problem. Together, they came up with a plan.

Benny and a group of beavers would travel downstream to the human dam. They would gnaw at the base of the dam and weaken it, so the water could flow freely again. The other beavers would stay behind and keep an eye on the Great Dam.

The journey was long and hard, but Benny and his group of beavers were determined. They swam for hours, and finally, they arrived at the human dam. They set to work, gnawing away at the base of the dam.

It was slow work, but Benny and the beavers were relentless. They gnawed and chewed, and finally, the dam started to crack. Water began to trickle through, and the beavers knew that they had succeeded.

Benny and the beavers returned to the Great Dam, tired but proud of their work. They had saved the brook, and they had shown that be

THE GREAT DAM BUILDER

STORY 2
THE HELPER HEDGEHOG:
A TALE OF KINDNESS AND
COMPASSION

Once upon a time, in a lush green forest,
there lived a hedgehog named Henry.
Henry was a very happy and content
hedgehog who loved nothing more than

rolling into a ball and sleeping under the stars. He had a cozy burrow in a hidden corner of the forest, and he loved spending his days exploring the forest and collecting shiny stones.

One day, as Henry was out on his usual walk, he heard a soft whimpering sound. It was coming from behind a large tree. Curious, Henry rolled into a ball and crept closer to investigate. As he came closer, he saw a little bird that had fallen from its nest.

The bird looked up at Henry with pleading eyes. "Please help me," it said weakly. "I can't fly, and my family is far away."

Henry felt a sudden surge of compassion for the little bird. He knew that he had to help. So he uncurled himself and gently picked up the bird in his quills. He cradled the bird in his soft underbelly and started to make his way back to his burrow.

As they walked, the bird started to tell Henry about its family and the great migration they were making. But the little bird was too weak to continue. Henry knew he had to help the bird get back to its family, so he decided to carry the bird on his back.

For the next few days, Henry carried the bird on his back through the forest. He braved the wind and rain, and he never once complained. He was determined to help the little bird get back to its family.

Finally, they arrived at a large tree, and Henry knew that they had found the bird's family. The little bird chirped with joy as it recognized its family. Henry gently placed the bird on the tree and watched as it was welcomed back with open wings.

The bird's family was overjoyed to see their

little one again, and they knew that they had Henry to thank. They invited him to stay and rest for a while, and they showered him with gifts of shiny stones and berries.

Henry was touched by their kindness, and he knew that he had made some new friends. But he also knew that it was time for him to return to his burrow. So he said his goodbyes and started to make his way back home.

As he walked, Henry thought about how good it had felt to help the little bird. He realized that he had a gift for helping others and that he wanted to use that gift to make a difference in the world.

And so, Henry decided to become a helper to anyone who needed it. He became known as the forest's resident helper, always ready to lend a hand to anyone in need. He helped other animals build their homes, collect food, and even rescued a few other birds who had fallen from their nests.

Word of Henry's kindness and helpfulness quickly spread throughout the forest, and he soon became a beloved figure. He was known as the hedgehog who would do anything for anyone.

Years went by, and Henry grew old. But he never lost his spirit of kindness and his desire to help others. He was loved by all the creatures of the forest, and he knew that he had made a difference in the world.

One day, as Henry was sleeping in his burrow, he heard a soft chirping sound. It was the little bird he had helped all those years ago. The bird had grown up and started its own family, and it had come to say thank you to Henry.

The bird told Henry that his kindness had inspired it to help others, and that it was now known as the most helpful bird in the forest. Henry was touched by the bird's words, and he knew that he

THE SELFISH BADGER'S REDEMPTION

Once upon a time, in a deep and dense forest, there lived a badger named Bart. Bart was a very grumpy and selfish badger who loved nothing more than hoarding food in his cozy burrow. He had a reputation in the forest for being the most selfish and unhelpful creature around.

One day, as Bart was digging through the dirt in search of food, he heard a faint noise coming from a nearby tree. Curious, he waddled over to the tree and saw a small bird with a broken wing perched on one of the branches.

The little bird looked up at Bart with pleading eyes. "Please help me," it said weakly. "I can't fly, and I need to get back to my family."

Bart didn't care about the bird's family or its problems. All he cared about was himself and his food. So he snarled at the bird and walked away, muttering to himself about how he didn't have time for other creatures' problems.

But as he walked away, he couldn't shake the feeling of guilt that had washed over

him. For the first time in his life, Bart felt a sense of shame for his selfishness. He realized that he had been wrong to ignore the little bird's plea for help.

Bart knew that he had to make things right. So he turned around and went back to the tree where the little bird was perched. He gently picked up the bird in his strong claws and carried it back to his burrow.

For the next few days, Bart took care of the little bird. He fed it worms and berries and kept it warm and safe in his burrow. And as he took care of the bird, he started to feel a sense of joy that he had never felt before.

As the little bird's wing healed, it started to sing songs of joy and gratitude. Bart listened to the bird's beautiful songs, and he realized that he had never truly appreciated the beauty of the forest around him.

When the little bird's wing had fully healed, Bart knew that it was time to take it back to its family. He walked the little bird all the way back to its tree and watched as it was welcomed back with open wings.

The little bird's family was overjoyed to see their little one again, and they knew that they had Bart to thank. They invited him to stay and rest for a while, and they shared their food and stories with him.

Bart was touched by their kindness, and he realized that he had been missing out on so much by being selfish and unhelpful. He decided to make a change and become a more kind and giving badger.

And so, Bart started to help the other creatures in the forest. He helped the squirrels gather nuts, the rabbits dig burrows, and the birds build nests. He became known as the forest's resident helper, always ready to lend a hand to anyone in need.

Word of Bart's kindness and helpfulness quickly spread throughout the forest, and he soon became a beloved figure. He was no longer the grumpy and selfish badger, but a caring and helpful one.

Years went by, and Bart grew old. But he never lost his spirit of kindness and his desire to help others. He was loved by all the creatures of the forest, and he knew that he had made a difference in the world.

One day, as Bart was sleeping in his burrow, he heard a soft tapping sound. It was the little bird he had helped all those years ago. The bird had grown up and started its own family, and it had come to say thank you to Bart.

The bird told Bart that his kindness had inspired it to help others, and that it was now known as

THE LEGACY OF DARIA, PROTECTOR OF THE FOREST

In the heart of a vast, green forest, there

lived a gentle deer named Daria.

She was the most graceful and kind
creature in the forest, known for her beauty

and her gentle spirit. Every day, Daria would wander through the forest, stopping to nibble on the sweet grass and wildflowers.

One day, as she was grazing, Daria heard a cry for help. She followed the sound and discovered a small rabbit that was trapped in a thorn bush. The rabbit was scared and alone, and it was clear that it couldn't escape on its own.

Without hesitation, Daria carefully pulled the thorns away from the rabbit's fur and gently lifted it out of the bush. She cradled the little rabbit in her strong but gentle hooves and brought it back to her meadow, where she could keep it safe and feed it.

From that day on, Daria became known as the protector of the forest. She helped any creature that needed her help, from the smallest ant to the largest bear. She was kind and gentle, but also strong and brave.

One day, a group of hunters came into the forest. They were loud and dangerous, and they carried weapons that could harm any creature in their path. Daria knew that she had to protect her forest, so she gathered all the animals and led them into hiding.

The hunters searched high and low for their prey, but they couldn't find a single creature. They grew frustrated and angry, and they started to destroy the forest in their search for game.

Daria watched as the hunters cut down trees and polluted the streams. She knew that she had to do something to stop them, but she didn't know what to do.

Finally, she had an idea. She led the hunters to a part of the forest that was full of thorn bushes and treacherous paths. The hunters fell into traps and got lost in the thorns, and they soon realized that they were no match for the power of the forest.

In the end, the hunters gave up and left the forest. Daria was hailed as a hero, and she knew that she had protected her home and her family.

Years went by, and Daria grew old. She knew that it was time for her to pass on the mantle of protector to a new generation of animals. She called a meeting of all the animals in the forest and told them that it was time for them to take on the role of protector.

At first, the animals were scared and unsure. They didn't know if they had what it took to be a protector. But Daria told them that they were all strong and brave, and that they had the power to protect their home.

With Daria's guidance, the animals of the forest banded together and took on the role of protectors. They patrolled the forest and kept an eye out for danger. They worked together to keep their home safe and clean.

Daria watched as the animals grew and flourished. She was proud of the creatures that she had protected for so many years, and she knew that she had left a legacy of kindness and bravery.

One day, as Daria was lying in the meadow, she heard a soft rustling sound. She looked up and saw a group of young fawns playing in the grass. They were full of energy and joy, and they reminded her of herself when she was young.

Daria smiled as she watched the fawns. She knew that they would grow up to be strong and brave protectors, just like she had been. And she was grateful to have had the chance to pass on her legacy to a new generation of animals.

As the sun set over the forest, Daria closed her eyes and took her final breath. She had lived

THE LYNX AND THE KITTEN: A TALE OF COURAGE AND KINDNESS IN THE FOREST

In the deep, dark forests of the north, there lived a majestic lynx named Kaida. She was a creature beauty and grace, with sleek fur the color of freshly fallen snow and piercing green eyes that seemed to glow in the moonlight.

Kaida lived a solitary life, hunting for her meals and wandering through the forest in search of adventure. She was a fierce hunter, skilled at tracking her prey and leaping through the trees with effortless grace.

One day, as Kaida was out on a hunt, she heard a faint sound coming from a nearby grove of trees. It was a tiny, helpless cry, and Kaida knew that she had to investigate.

She crept quietly through the trees, following the sound of the cry. As she got closer, she saw a small kitten, its fur matted and tangled, and its eyes filled with fear.

Without hesitation, Kaida scooped up the kitten in her jaws and carried it back to her den. She cared for the kitten, cleaning its fur and feeding it with fresh meat.

Over the next few weeks, Kaida and the kitten grew close. The kitten, named Luna, followed Kaida everywhere she went, and Kaida taught Luna how to hunt and survive in the wild.

As the years went by, Kaida and Luna became inseparable. They roamed through the forest together, hunting and playing and exploring the wilderness. Kaida was happy to have Luna by her side, and Luna was grateful to have such a strong and wise mentor.

One day, as they were out on a hunt, Kaida and Luna heard a faint cry for help. They followed the sound and discovered a pack of wolves attacking a family of deer.

Kaida knew that they had to act fast. She leaped into action, using her sharp claws and quick reflexes to fend off the wolves and protect the deer. Luna helped too, using her small size and speed to distract the wolves and keep them away from the deer.

In the end, Kaida and Luna emerged victorious. The wolves retreated, and the deer family was safe. The deer thanked Kaida and Luna for their bravery and kindness, and Kaida realized that there was more to life than just hunting and wandering through the forest.

From that day on, Kaida and Luna became known as the protectors of the forest. They watched over the animals and kept them safe from harm, using their strength and courage to defend the weak and vulnerable.

As the years went by, Kaida grew old and her fur became gray with age. She knew that her time was coming to an end, but she was grateful for the life she had led and the lessons she had learned.

One day, as Kaida was lying in her den, she heard a soft rustling sound. She looked up and saw Luna, now grown and strong, with her own pack of kittens following her through the trees.

Kaida smiled as she watched Luna and her kittens. She knew that they would continue her legacy, using their strength and courage to protect the forest and keep it safe for all its creatures.

As the sun set over the forest, Kaida closed her eyes and took her final breath. She had lived a long and full life, and she knew that her spirit would live on in the hearts of all those who had known her.

Luna and her kittens continued Kaida's legacy, protecting the forest and keeping it safe for all its creatures. And though Kaida was gone, her memory lived on, a symbol of courage, strength, and kindness in the heart of the forest.

Fiona felt a sense of pride and joy as she watched the young birds grow and thrive. She knew that she had made a difference in their lives, just as she had made a difference in the lives of the other birds in the flock.

THE KINDHEARTED BEAR: A TALE OF COMPASSION IN THE FOREST

In the heart of a dense forest, a brown bear named Bruno lived with his family. Bruno was a large and strong bear with thick, brown fur and sharp claws. He spent most of his days fishing in the river and foraging for berries and nuts in the forest.

One day, Bruno was out on a hunt when he heard a strange noise coming from a nearby clearing. He followed the sound and found a small, frightened rabbit caught in a trap.

Bruno's first instinct was to ignore the rabbit and continue his hunt, but something about the rabbit's desperate cries tugged at his heartstrings. He approached the rabbit and used his massive strength to free it from the trap.

The rabbit, grateful for Bruno's kindness, hopped around him in circles, thanking him profusely. Bruno was taken aback by the rabbit's gratitude and realized that there was more to life than just hunting and foraging.

Over the next few days, Bruno kept thinking about the rabbit and how it had made him feel. He decided that he wanted to help other animals in need, and so he began to explore the forest in search of creatures that he could assist.

One day, as he was wandering through the forest, Bruno heard a loud buzzing sound. He followed the sound and discovered a group of bees that were in danger of losing their hive to a nearby fire.

Bruno sprang into action, using his strength to move fallen trees and create a barrier to protect the hive from the flames. The bees were grateful for Bruno's quick thinking and bravery, and they rewarded him with a jar of their sweetest honey.

As the days went by, Bruno became known as a hero in the forest. Animals from all over came to him with their problems, and Bruno used his strength and ingenuity to help them in any way he could.

One day, a family of raccoons came to Bruno in tears. Their home had been destroyed in a storm, and they had nowhere to go. Bruno immediately took them in, offering them shelter in his own den and teaching them how to survive in the forest.

As the years went by, Bruno continued to help the animals of the forest, earning their love and respect. He had learned that sometimes, the most important thing in life is to help others, and he was grateful for the chance to make a difference in the world.

One winter, the forest was hit by a terrible blizzard. The snow was so deep that many of the animals were unable to leave their dens to find food. Bruno, recognizing the danger, sprang into action.

He spent his days trudging through the

snow, searching for animals in need and delivering food and supplies to those who were trapped. He even dug out the dens of the smaller animals, making sure that they had enough space to survive the cold winter.

Despite his tireless efforts, Bruno began to feel weak and tired. He knew that he was getting old, and that his days were numbered. But he also knew that he had made a difference in the world, and that he had helped many animals during his time in the forest.

As the snow began to melt, Bruno lay down in his den, his body weak and his breath shallow. He closed his eyes, surrounded by the warmth and love of his family and friends.

As the sun set over the forest, Bruno took his final breath, his heart filled with gratitude for the life he had lived and the animals he had helped. The forest was never quite the same after he was gone, but his memory lived on, a testament to the power of kindness and the importance of helping those in need.

SAMMY THE SINGING SQUIRREL: A FOREST LEGEND

In a forest full of tall trees and wild animals, a small squirrel named Sammy lived a quiet life. Sammy was small, even for a squirrel, but he was fast, nimble, and clever. He spent most of his days running up and

down the trees, gathering nuts and berries for the winter ahead.

Sammy was a good-natured squirrel, always willing to help his friends and family. He would share his food with others and teach young squirrels how to climb trees and gather nuts. But despite his friendly nature, Sammy often felt like he was invisible in the forest, unnoticed by the larger animals and overlooked by his fellow squirrels.

One day, as Sammy was running up a tree, he heard a strange sound. It was a soft, melodic tune, unlike anything he had ever heard before. Intrigued, he followed the sound, hopping from tree to tree until he reached a small clearing in the forest.

There, sitting on a stump, was a beautiful bird with bright blue feathers and a melodious voice. She was singing a song that echoed through the forest, drawing in animals from all around.

Sammy was entranced by the bird's song. He had never heard anything so beautiful in his life. As the bird finished her song, Sammy ran up to her, his heart beating fast.

"That was amazing!" he said. "I've never heard anything like it."

The bird looked at Sammy with a kind smile. "Thank you," she said. "I love to sing, and I'm always happy to share my songs with others."

Sammy and the bird spent the rest of the day together, talking and laughing and sharing stories. Sammy felt like he had found a kindred spirit in the bird, someone who understood him and appreciated him for who he was.

Over the next few days, Sammy visited the

bird in the clearing every chance he got. He would watch her sing, mesmerized by the beauty of her voice, and they would talk for hours about everything under the sun.

As Sammy spent more time with the bird, he began to notice a change in himself. He felt more confident and sure of himself, as though he had found a purpose in life beyond just gathering nuts and berries. He began to sing along with the bird, and he even started to write his own songs.

But as the days went by, Sammy began to realize that the bird was not like the other animals in the forest. She was not bound to the ground like he was; she could fly away whenever she wanted. And one day, she did just that.

Sammy was devastated. He had grown so close to the bird, and he didn't know how to go on without her. For days, he moped around the forest, feeling lost and alone.

But then he realized something. The bird had given him a gift, something that he had been searching for his entire life. She had given him the gift of music, and Sammy knew that he could use that gift to make a difference in the forest.

He began to sing his own songs, and soon, other animals in the forest began to take notice. They would gather around Sammy as he sang, entranced by the beauty of his voice and the passion in his songs.

Sammy had found his purpose in life. He may have been small, but he had a gift that could bring joy to others. And in that way, he had become a giant in the forest, a source of inspiration and hope for all who knew him.

Years passed, and Sammy grew old. But his voice never faded. He continued to sing his songs, and the animals of the forest continued to gather around him, entranced by his talent and his spirit.

One day, as Sammy lay down in his den

STORY 8
THE SECRET MEADOW'S LOVE

In a forest nestled between rolling hills and trickling streams, a little red fox named Finn

lived a life full of adventure and mischief.

He was always on the move, darting

through the undergrowth and leaping over fallen logs, looking for his next thrill.

Finn was the youngest of his family, and he had always been a bit of a troublemaker. He loved to play pranks on his siblings, and he was always getting into scraps with the other animals in the forest. But despite his rambunctious nature, Finn was well-loved by all who knew him. His quick wit and infectious laugh made him the life of the party.

One day, as Finn was exploring the woods, he stumbled upon a secret meadow hidden deep in the heart of the forest. The meadow was unlike anything Finn had ever seen before. It was full of wildflowers and tall grasses, and a cool stream ran through the center. But what caught Finn's eye the most was the tree in the center of the meadow, a giant oak with branches that stretched up to the sky.

Finn was a bit of a climber, and he couldn't resist the urge to climb the tree. He scampered up the trunk, his claws gripping the rough bark as he ascended higher and higher. When he reached the top, he was amazed by the view. He could see the entire forest from up there, and the world seemed so much bigger and more beautiful than he had ever imagined.

As Finn sat there, basking in the beauty of the meadow and the tree, he heard a sound. It was a soft rustling, like someone moving through the grass below. Finn looked down and saw a rabbit hopping through the meadow, her long ears twitching as she nibbled on a blade of grass.

Finn was struck by the rabbit's beauty. She was sleek and graceful, with fur the color of cream and eyes like dark chocolate. He felt a flutter in his chest, a feeling he had never experienced before.

Finn watched the rabbit for a long time, mesmerized by her every move. He didn't know what to do or say, but he knew that he wanted to be near her.

As the days went by, Finn spent more and more time in the secret meadow. He would climb the oak tree and watch the rabbit as she hopped through the grass. He never spoke to her, but he felt a connection with her that he couldn't explain.

But one day, something changed. Finn was sitting in the oak tree, watching the rabbit as she nibbled on a clover, when he heard a sound that made his heart race. It was the sound of a hunter's horn, and it was coming from deep within the forest. Finn knew that hunters could be dangerous, and he didn't want the rabbit to be hurt. He knew that he had to do something to protect her.

He climbed down the tree and darted through the meadow, dodging between the wildflowers as he raced towards the rabbit. When he reached her, he nudged her with his nose, urging her to follow him.

The rabbit was hesitant at first, but when she saw the fear in Finn's eyes, she knew that she had to trust him. She hopped after him, her heart racing as they ran through the forest.

Finn led the rabbit to a hidden burrow in the side of a hill. It was a cozy little den, with soft grasses and leaves piled up for bedding. Finn urged the rabbit to climb inside, and he curled up next to her, his body a warm shield against the cold. As they lay there, Finn realized that he had fallen in love with the rabbit. He had never felt such

GUARDIAN OF THE WOODS: THE POWERFUL AND VIGILANT MOUFLON

In the heart of a great forest, high up in the mountains, there lived a magnificent creature named Max. Max was a mouflon, a wild sheep with a thick coat of shaggy hair and a pair of magnificent horns. Max was proud of his horns, which he had polished to a high shine, and he was always eager to show them off to anyone who would take notice.

But Max was not just about his looks. He was a strong and powerful animal, with sharp hooves and a keen sense of smell. He could run for miles through the forest without getting tired, and he was an expert at finding the best food and water sources.

Max was the leader of his herd, a group of mouflons who looked up to him for guidance and protection. He took his responsibilities seriously, and he was always

on the lookout for any danger that might threaten his herd.

One day, while Max and his herd were grazing on a hillside, they heard a loud noise coming from the forest below. It was a sound they had never heard before, and it made Max's heart race. He knew that he had to investigate.

He called out to his herd, urging them to follow him, and he led them down the hill towards the source of the noise. As they neared the forest, Max could see that there was a large truck parked on the edge of the trees. It was filled with hunters, their guns at the ready, and they were making their way through the forest, searching for prey.

Max knew that he had to act fast. He called out to his herd, urging them to scatter and hide, and he made his way towards the hunters. His horns glinted in the sunlight, and his hooves pounded the ground as he charged towards the truck.

The hunters were surprised by Max's sudden appearance, and they raised their guns in defense. But Max was quick and agile, and he darted between them, his horns missing their mark by inches. The hunters were scared by Max's power and speed, and they quickly retreated back to their truck.

Max was relieved that he had been able to scare off the hunters, but he knew that he couldn't let his guard down. He called out to his herd, urging them to stay hidden and to be on the lookout for any more hunters that might come their way.

Days passed, and Max kept watch over his herd. He made sure that they had enough food and water, and he kept a keen eye out for any signs of danger. But despite his vigilance, he could not shake the feeling that something was amiss.

One night, as Max was grazing on a hillside, he saw a group of hunters making their way through the forest towards his herd. They were carrying rifles, and they had a pack of hunting dogs with them. Max knew that he had to act fast.

He called out to his herd, urging them to run, and he made his way towards the hunters. His horns glinted in the moonlight, and his hooves pounded the ground as he charged towards the hunters.

The hunters were prepared this time, and they raised their guns in defense. But Max was not afraid. He charged towards them, his horns aimed straight at the hunters' guns. The hunters fired their guns, but Max was too quick, and he dodged the bullets with ease.

Max's horns hit the hunters' guns, knocking them out of their hands, and the hunters ran away in fear. The hunting dogs barked and yelped, but they were no match for

Max's strength and speed. He chased them deep into the forest, making sure that they would never come back.

Max was relieved that he had been able to protect his herd, but he knew that he

STORY 10
GUARDIAN OF THE FOREST: BRUNO, THE POWERFUL PROTECTOR

In a dense forest, deep in the heart of the countryside, there lived a wild boar named Bruno. Bruno was a fierce and powerful animal, with a thick coat of bristly hair and a pair of sharp tusks that he would use to

defend himself from any danger that might come his way. He was the king of the forest, and all the other animals looked up to him with respect and awe.

Bruno was proud of his strength and power, but he was also a kind and gentle soul. He would never harm another animal unless he was threatened, and he was always eager to help out any animal in need. He was the protector of the forest, and he took his responsibilities very seriously.

One day, while Bruno was out foraging for food, he heard a strange noise coming from the edge of the forest. It was a sound he had never heard before, and it made his heart race. He knew that he had to investigate.

He made his way towards the noise, his tusks at the ready, and he saw a group of hunters making their way through the forest towards him. They were carrying rifles, and they had a pack of hunting dogs with them. Bruno knew that he had to act fast.

He called out to his fellow animals, urging them to hide, and he made his way towards the hunters. His tusks glinted in the sunlight, and his hooves pounded the ground as he charged towards the hunters.

The hunters were prepared this time, and they raised their guns in defense. But Bruno was not afraid. He charged towards them, his tusks aimed straight at the hunters' guns. The hunters fired their guns, but Bruno was too quick, and he dodged the bullets with ease.

Bruno's tusks hit the hunters' guns, knocking them out of their hands, and the hunters ran away in fear. The hunting dogs barked and yelped, but they were no match for Bruno's strength and speed. He chased them deep into the forest, making sure that they would never come back.

Bruno was relieved that he had been able to protect his fellow animals, but he knew that he couldn't let his guard down. He called out to the animals, urging them to stay hidden and to be on the lookout for any more hunters that might come their way.

Days passed, and Bruno kept watch over the forest. He made sure that the animals had enough food and water, and he kept a keen eye out for any signs of danger. But despite his vigilance, he could not shake the feeling that something was amiss.

One night, as Bruno was out foraging for food, he saw a group of hunters making their way through the forest towards his herd. They were carrying rifles, and they had a pack of hunting dogs with them. Bruno knew that he had to act fast.

He called out to his herd, urging them to run, and he made his way towards the hunters. His tusks glinted in the moonlight, and his hooves pounded the ground as he charged towards the hunters.

The hunters were prepared this time, and they raised their guns in defense. But Bruno was not afraid. He charged towards them, his tusks aimed straight at the hunters' guns. The hunters fired their guns, but Bruno was too quick, and he dodged the bullets with ease.

Bruno's tusks hit the hunters' guns, knocking them out of their hands, and the hunters ran away in fear. The hunting dogs barked and yelped, but they were no match for Bruno's strength and speed. He chased them deep into the forest, making sure that they would never come back.

Bruno was relieved that he had been able to protect his herd, but he knew

THE POWER OF HELPING OTHERS: A STORY OF ANIMAL COMMUNITY AND KINDNESS

Once upon a time, in a magical forest far away, lived a group of animals who all got along well with each other. They spent their days playing, exploring the forest and helping each other out whenever they could.

In this forest, there lived a wise old owl named Oliver. He was the most respected animal in the forest because he was the one who had all the answers. Whenever the animals had a problem or a question, they would go to him for advice. He was always happy to help and his words of wisdom never failed to inspire the animals.

One day, the animals gathered around Oliver and asked him, "Oliver, what is the

secret to living a happy and fulfilling life?"

Oliver looked at them and said, "The secret to a happy life is to always be kind, compassionate, and helpful to others. The more you help others, the happier you will be."

The animals were intrigued by Oliver's advice, and they decided to put it to the test. They all agreed to help each other out, no matter what.

The first animal to need help was a little mouse named Mickey. Mickey was always getting lost in the forest and couldn't find his way back home. The other animals would often help him find his way back, but this time was different. They decided to take turns looking after him and making sure he didn't get lost. This way, he would always have someone with him and he would never feel alone.

The next animal to need help was a bird named Sammy. Sammy had a broken wing and couldn't fly. The other animals knew that Sammy loved to fly and it made him very sad that he couldn't do it anymore. They decided to build a special flying machine that would help Sammy fly again. They worked together to build the machine, and when it was finished, they took Sammy on a flight over the forest. Sammy was thrilled, and the other animals were happy to see him happy.

The animals continued to help each other out in any way they could. They would gather food for the ones who couldn't find any, or help build nests for the birds who couldn't fly. They even helped the little insects cross the river by building a bridge so they wouldn't get washed away by the water.

As the days went by, the animals became happier and happier. They had found a sense of purpose in helping each other out. They realized that when they helped others, it gave them a sense of joy and fulfillment that they had never experienced before.

One day, the animals decided to have a celebration to thank Oliver for his wise words of advice. They gathered around him and presented him with a gift. It was a beautiful crystal that shone brightly in the sunlight.

Oliver was very pleased with their gift, and he said, "This crystal represents the kindness, compassion, and love that you have shown each other. It is a symbol of your strength as a community, and a reminder that you can achieve anything if you work together and help each other out."

The animals were proud of themselves and each other. They had become a strong and loving community, and they knew that they could always count on each other for help and support.

And so, the animals continued to live in the forest, helping each other out and spreading love and kindness wherever they went. They knew that they had found the secret to a happy and fulfilling life, and they never forgot the wise words of Oliver, the old owl.

STORY 12
THE ANIMAL TEAM: USING THEIR UNIQUE TALENTS TO HELP OTHERS IN THE FOREST

Once upon a time, in a dense forest, there lived a group of animals who were the best of friends. Among them were a rabbit, a squirrel, a bear, a fox, and a deer. They all lived together in a peaceful harmony and helped each other in times of need.

One day, as the animals were gathered around the watering hole, they heard a loud noise coming from the nearby bushes. They quickly made their way towards the noise, and there they found a tiny bird who had fallen from her nest.

The animals were concerned for the bird's safety and quickly helped her back to her nest. They knew that the bird's mother would be worried and so they decided to keep an eye on her until her mother returned.

As they waited, the animals got to talking and realized that they all had unique talents and abilities. The rabbit was quick and nimble, the squirrel was an expert climber, the bear was strong and fearless, the fox was cunning and clever, and the deer had keen senses.

They decided to form a team and use their skills to help other animals in need. The rabbit would lead the way, the squirrel would climb trees to get a better view, the bear would protect them from any danger, the fox would use her intelligence to solve problems, and the deer would use her senses to detect any danger.

Their first mission was to help a family of otters who were in danger of losing their home. The otters had built their dam across a river, but it was in danger of collapsing due to a heavy rainfall.

The animal team quickly made their way to the river and saw that the otters were in a tough spot. The water was rising, and the dam was beginning to crack. If it collapsed, the otters would be swept away, and their home would be destroyed.

The bear quickly got to work, using his strength to reinforce the dam. The squirrel climbed up to get a better view, while the rabbit ran back and forth, alerting the others to any potential dangers. The fox used her intelligence to come up with a solution, and the deer used her senses to detect any potential problems.

Together, they worked tirelessly, and eventually, they were able to save the otters' home. The otters were overjoyed and thanked the animal team for their help.

From that day on, the animal team became well-known throughout the forest for their good deeds. They helped a family of beavers build a new dam, rescued a group of baby birds who had fallen from their nest, and even helped a lost baby deer find its way back to its mother.

The animals had found a new sense of

purpose and fulfillment in helping others. They were no longer just friends but had become protectors of the forest, using their unique talents and abilities to make a positive difference in the lives of others.

And whenever they were faced with a difficult situation, they would remind themselves of the time when they had saved the otters' home. It had been a challenging task, but they had worked together and had succeeded. They had learned that working together, using each other's strengths, is the key to solving any problem.

And so, the animal team continued to help others, spreading love and kindness throughout the forest. They had become a shining example of what can be achieved when animals work together towards a common goal.

THE LEGACY OF GREY: A WOLF'S FIGHT TO PROTECT THE FOREST

Once upon a time, in a dense forest in the mountains, lived a pack of wolves. Among the pack was a lone wolf who was larger than the others, with a thick coat of fur and piercing amber eyes. His name was Grey, and he was a respected member of the pack, known for his cunning and his prowess in hunting.

Grey had lived for over 900 years, and he had seen the forest change over time. He had seen the trees grow taller, the rivers flow faster, and the animals come and go. He had also seen the humans come into the forest, building roads and houses and disrupting the natural balance.

One day, Grey was out hunting when he came across a human settlement. He watched from afar as the humans went about their daily lives, chopping down trees

and polluting the river.

He knew that something had to be done to protect the forest and its creatures.

Grey returned to the pack and called for a meeting. He spoke to them about the humans and their destructive ways, and he suggested that they form an alliance with the other animals in the forest to protect their home.

At first, the other wolves were hesitant. They had always kept to themselves, and they were wary of the other animals in the forest. But Grey was persistent, and he knew that this was the only way to protect the forest.

Over time, Grey began to meet with the other animals in the forest. He spoke to the bears, the deer, and the rabbits, and he convinced them that they all had a stake in protecting the forest. They agreed to form an alliance, and together they worked to protect the forest from the humans.

The alliance was not without its challenges.

There were disagreements between the different species, and there were moments when they thought they might not be able to work together. But Grey was always there to remind them of their common goal, and he worked tirelessly to keep the alliance together.

As the years went by, the alliance grew stronger, and they were able to push back against the humans. They protested against the cutting down of trees, and they worked to clean up the pollution in the river. They also worked to educate the humans about the importance of protecting the forest and its creatures.

The humans were not always receptive to their message, but Grey never gave up. He knew that their efforts were making a difference, and he was proud of what they had accomplished.

One day, Grey was out hunting with the pack when they came across a group of humans who were poaching in the forest. The wolves were outraged, and they attacked the humans to protect the animals that they had come to know and love.

The humans fought back, and Grey was gravely injured in the fight. The other animals in the forest came to his aid, and together they were able to drive the humans out of the forest.

Grey was grateful for their help, and he knew that he had to do something to repay them. He spoke to the other wolves, and together they came up with a plan. They decided to build a sanctuary in the forest where the animals could live in peace and safety.

The sanctuary was a success, and it became a symbol of hope for the animals in the forest. Grey knew that he had made a difference, and he was proud of the legacy that he had left behind.

In the end, Grey passed away, but his memory lived on in the forest. The wolves, the bears, the deer, and the rabbits all remembered the brave wolf who had fought to protect their home, and they knew that they would continue to honor his legacy for generations to come.

THE FLYING FROG: A TALE OF TRANSFORMATION AND COURAGE

Once upon a time, in a small pond in the middle of a vast meadow, lived a small

green frog named Freddy.

Freddy was a curious and adventurous frog,

always exploring the pond and its surroundings.

One day, as he was hopping along the pond, he noticed something strange. There was a large rock in the middle of the pond that he had never seen before. As he got closer, he realized that it wasn't a rock at all, but a turtle!

Freddy had never seen a turtle before, and he was both fascinated and a little scared. He decided to approach the turtle slowly, making sure not to startle it.

To Freddy's surprise, the turtle was friendly and greeted him warmly. His name was Timmy, and he had been living in the pond for many years. Timmy and Freddy quickly became friends, and Timmy showed Freddy around the pond, introducing him to the other creatures who lived there.

Freddy was especially fascinated by the

dragonflies that darted above the pond's surface, and he spent hours watching them fly. He dreamed of flying like them, but he knew that as a frog, he was grounded.

One day, as Freddy was lounging on a lily pad, he noticed something unusual in the water. It was a small fish, struggling to swim against the current. Freddy knew that the fish was in danger, so he quickly hopped into the water and swam over to help.

Using his strong legs, Freddy pushed against the current and guided the fish to safety. The fish was grateful and thanked Freddy for his help. From that day on, Freddy became the protector of the pond, always keeping an eye out for creatures in need.

But Freddy still longed to fly, and he couldn't help but feel a little envious of the dragonflies. He asked Timmy if he had ever seen a frog fly before, and Timmy shook his head.

"Frogs can't fly, Freddy," he said. "It's just not possible."

But Freddy refused to give up on his dream. He spent hours watching the dragonflies, studying their wings and their movements. He even started practicing jumping higher and higher, hoping that he could somehow launch himself into the air.

One day, as he was practicing his jumps, he noticed that something strange was happening. His jumps were getting higher and higher, and he felt lighter than he ever had before.

Suddenly, he realized what was happening. He was transforming into a tree frog! His body was changing, and he could feel his legs elongating and his skin turning a bright yellow.

At first, Freddy was scared, but then he realized that this was his chance to fly. He took a deep breath and leaped into the air, flapping his new wings as he went.

To his amazement, he was flying! He soared through the air, feeling the wind in his face and the sun on his back. He felt free, like he could go anywhere he wanted.

Freddy landed back in the pond, exhilarated by his experience. He knew that he had a special gift, and he vowed to use it to help others. He became the protector of the pond and its surroundings, flying above the trees and keeping a watchful eye out for any dangers.

Years went by, and Freddy became known throughout the meadow as the flying frog. He was respected and loved by all the creatures who lived there, and he was always ready to help those in need.

One day, as he was flying over the meadow, he saw something that made him stop in his tracks. A group of humans was approaching the pond, carrying nets and fishing rods.

Freddy knew that the humans meant trouble. He flew back to the pond and sounded

STORY 15
BENNY THE LITTLE BROWN BAT: FROM CURIOUS EXPLORER TO NIGHT FLYER AND PROTECTOR

Once upon a time, in a dark cave nestled in the mountains, lived a little brown bat named Benny. Benny was a curious bat, always eager to explore the depths of the cave and the world beyond.

One evening, as he was fluttering around the cave, Benny noticed something strange. A group of humans had set up camp outside the cave, and they were carrying strange contraptions that emitted bright lights and loud noises.

Benny was curious but also a little scared. He had never seen humans before, and he wasn't sure what they were capable of. He decided to approach them cautiously, making sure to stay out of sight.

To his surprise, the humans were friendly and greeted him warmly. They were scientists, studying the bats that lived in the cave. They had set up cameras and microphones to observe the bats' behavior and record their sounds.

Benny was fascinated by the humans and their equipment. He watched as they

analyzed the data they had collected, and he even allowed them to attach a small transmitter to his back so they could track his movements.

Over the next few weeks, Benny became a regular visitor to the human camp. He would flutter in and out of the cave, observing the humans and their equipment. He even started to recognize some of the scientists by their voices and scents.

But Benny's curiosity didn't stop there. He also became interested in the world beyond the cave. He would often fly out of the cave at night, exploring the surrounding mountains and forests.

One night, as he was flying over the mountains, Benny noticed something unusual. There was a group of bats flying in a strange pattern, swooping and diving in a way that he had never seen before.

Benny was curious and decided to join them. He followed their lead, mimicking their movements and trying to keep up with their speed.

To his surprise, he found that he was a natural. He was able to fly with ease, effortlessly following the other bats and feeling the wind rushing past him.

He realized that he had found a new community, a group of bats that shared his love of exploration and adventure. They called themselves the Night Flyers, and Benny was thrilled to be a part of them.

As a member of the Night Flyers, Benny learned many new skills. He learned how to hunt for insects, how to navigate by echolocation, and how to communicate with other bats using a complex system of sounds and calls.

But most importantly, he learned how to work together as a team. The Night Flyers were a tight-knit group, always looking out for one another and working together to achieve their goals.

One night, as they were flying over the forest, they noticed something unusual. A group of humans had set up a large net, blocking the path of a group of migrating birds.

The Night Flyers knew that they had to help. They swooped down and began to distract the humans, fluttering around them and emitting high-pitched screeches.

The humans were confused and scared, and they quickly packed up their equipment and left the area. The Night Flyers had saved the birds, and they felt a sense of pride and accomplishment.

Benny realized that he had found his true

calling. He was not just a curious bat, but a protector of the night, a guardian of the forest and all its creatures.

Years went by, and Benny became known throughout the forest as the Night Flyer. He was respected and loved by all the creatures who lived there, and he was always ready to help those in need.

And as he fluttered through the darkness, Benny knew that he had found his place in the world, soaring with the bats, protecting the night, and exploring the unknown.

BELLA'S ADVENTURE: A BUTTERFLY'S JOURNEY TO DISCOVER THE WORLD

In a lush green meadow, surrounded by tall trees and colorful flowers, lived a beautiful butterfly named Bella. Bella was a small, delicate creature with vibrant wings that shimmered in the sunlight.

She spent her days fluttering from flower to flower, sipping nectar and enjoying the warmth of the sun on her wings. She was happy and content, but she longed for something more.

Bella had always been fascinated by the world beyond the meadow. She had heard stories of vast oceans, towering mountains, and endless deserts. She yearned to explore these places, to see the world from a different perspective.

One day, as she was flying over the meadow, she noticed a group of butterflies flying in the distance. They were larger and more colorful than any butterfly she had ever seen before, and she felt a sudden urge to join them.

With a burst of excitement, Bella fluttered over to the group and introduced herself. They welcomed her warmly and explained that they were migrating to a warmer climate for the winter.

Bella was thrilled at the idea of embarking on such an adventure. She joined the group, and they set off on their journey, soaring high above the treetops and into the unknown.

As they flew over mountains and valleys, forests and deserts, Bella saw the world in a whole new light. She marveled at the beauty of the landscape, the diversity of the creatures that lived there, and the sheer vastness of it all.

But the journey was not without its challenges. One day, as they were flying over a vast ocean, a fierce storm blew in, and the winds whipped them around like leaves in a hurricane.

Bella was terrified, but she knew that she had to keep flying. She flapped her wings with all her might, struggling to stay airborne as the wind buffeted her from all sides.

Finally, after what felt like hours of flying, the storm passed, and the group landed on a small island in the middle of the ocean. They were exhausted and shaken, but they were also relieved to have made it through the storm alive.

As they rested on the island, Bella realized something. She had always thought of herself as fragile and delicate, but she had just survived one of the fiercest storms in the world. She had proven to herself that she was stronger than she had ever imagined.

The group continued on their journey, and after many weeks of flying, they finally arrived at their destination. They landed in a lush tropical forest, full of brightly colored flowers and fruit trees.

Bella felt a sense of accomplishment and joy. She had traveled to places that she had only dreamed of, and she had done it with the help of her new friends.

As winter passed, Bella enjoyed her new home, but she knew that she would eventually have to return to the meadow. She had missed her family and friends, and she wanted to share her adventures with them.

When spring came, Bella said goodbye to her new friends and set off on the long journey back to the meadow. As she flew over the familiar landscape, she felt a sense of nostalgia and joy.

When she finally arrived, she was greeted with open arms by her family and friends. She spent the rest of her days fluttering around the meadow, sipping nectar, and telling stories of her adventures.

But she also knew that there was a whole world out there waiting to be explored. And whenever she felt the urge to wander, she would spread her wings and take to the sky, ready for whatever adventure lay ahead.

THE SEA EAGLE WHO FOUGHT AGAINST HUMAN WASTE AND PROTECTS THE ECOSYSTEM

In the rugged coastline of the North Atlantic, where the wind and waves rage against the shore, a sea eagle named Sam soared over the choppy waters in search of

his next meal. Sam was a magnificent bird, with a wingspan of nearly seven feet and sharp talons that could snatch a fish from the water in a split second.

Sam was born in a nest high up in a rocky cliff overlooking the sea. He learned to fly and hunt from his parents, who taught him how to dive from great heights and snatch fish from the water. He was a quick learner, and soon he was catching fish on his own.

One day, as Sam was flying over the sea, he spotted a school of herring swimming just below the surface. He circled above them, scanning for the perfect opportunity to strike. Suddenly, he saw his chance. He dove from the sky, his wings tucked tight against his body, and plunged into the water with a loud splash.

Sam emerged from the water with a large herring clutched in his talons. He flapped his wings and soared back into the sky, feeling proud and satisfied.

But as he flew over the coastline, he noticed something strange. The sea was different than it had been before. The waves were choppier, and there was a strange smell in the air. He knew that something was wrong.

He flew closer to the shore and saw a group of humans standing on the beach. They were holding nets and poles and were shouting and waving their arms. Sam knew that they were fishermen, and that they were trying to catch fish.

But as he watched, he saw something that made his heart sink. One of the fishermen had caught a large fish, but instead of putting it in a basket, he threw it back into the water. Sam couldn't understand why anyone would waste such a valuable resource.

He flew closer to the fishermen and landed on a nearby rock. He looked at them with his sharp eyes and tried to understand what they were doing.

Suddenly, one of the fishermen noticed him and shouted, "Look, it's a sea eagle! Get your camera!"

Sam felt a pang of fear. He had heard stories of humans hunting eagles for their feathers and their talons. He didn't want to be caught, but he also didn't want to leave the area without figuring out what was going on.

He decided to stay and observe the humans, hoping to learn more about their activities. As he watched, he saw that they were using large nets to catch fish. They would haul in the nets, sort through the catch, and throw back anything that they didn't want.

Sam realized that the fishermen were only interested in catching a few types of fish, and that they were throwing back everything else, even if it was still alive.

He knew that this was wasteful and harmful to the ecosystem. He wanted to do something to help, but he didn't know how.

Over the next few days, Sam continued to observe the fishermen, trying to come up with a plan. He saw that they were taking more and more fish out of the sea, and that the fish populations were dwindling.

He knew that he had to act fast. He decided to use his skills as a hunter to catch some of the fish that the humans were throwing back into the water. He would take the fish to his nest and feed them to his young.

Sam started to spend more time near the fishermen, waiting for them to catch a fish that he could snatch from the water. He became more daring, diving closer to the nets and risking his safety to catch a meal.

But his efforts paid off. He caught enough fish to feed his family and was able to help reduce the amount of waste in the sea.

As time passed,

THE HUMMINGBIRD AND THE NEST: A TALE OF FRIENDSHIP AND FAMILY IN THE RAINFOREST

In a lush tropical rainforest, there lived a tiny hummingbird named Rosie. She was smaller than most of the other birds in the forest, but what she lacked in size, she made up for in speed and agility. Rosie's wings beat so fast that they made a humming sound, which is how she got her name.

Rosie lived in a beautiful part of the forest, filled with brightly colored flowers and juicy fruit trees. She loved to fly from flower to flower, sipping nectar and spreading pollen from one bloom to the next. She was always on the move, flitting around with her lightning-fast wings, never staying in one place for too long.

One day, as Rosie was flying through the forest, she spotted a small spider web in the path of a gust of wind. The web was home to a tiny spider, who had spent hours

spinning it with great care. Rosie knew that the spider's hard work was about to be ruined, and she decided to act.

She flew over to the web and hovered in

front of it, using her wings to create a breeze that would blow the web to safety. The spider was grateful and thanked Rosie for her help.

From that day on, the spider and Rosie became good friends. Rosie would often visit the spider's web, bringing her gifts of nectar and pollen. In return, the spider would keep the web clean and tidy, so that Rosie could fly through it without getting stuck.

Rosie continued to explore the forest, always seeking new adventures. She flew over streams and waterfalls, through the trees and over the mountains, and everywhere she went, she spread joy and beauty.

One day, as Rosie was flying through a part of the forest that she had never visited before, she heard a strange noise. It was a soft humming sound, like the beating of a thousand tiny wings. She followed the sound until she came to a small clearing, where she saw a group of hummingbirds hovering in the air.

The hummingbirds were of different colors and sizes, but they all had one thing in common: they were all working together to build a nest. Rosie watched in awe as they used twigs, leaves, and moss to construct a small but sturdy nest, high up in the trees.

She flew over to them and introduced herself, and soon she was welcomed into their community. She learned that they were a family of hummingbirds, working together to build a home for their babies.

Rosie was amazed at how hard the hummingbirds worked. They flew back and forth, carrying twigs and leaves in their beaks, weaving them together with great skill. They worked tirelessly, day and night, until the nest was complete.

When the nest was finished, the hummingbirds invited Rosie to see their eggs. They showed her three small white eggs, each about the size of a jelly bean. Rosie was fascinated by the eggs and asked the hummingbirds what they would do once the babies hatched.

The hummingbirds told Rosie that they would take turns caring for the babies. The mother would sit on the eggs to keep them warm, while the father would fly out to collect food. When the babies hatched, they would both work together to feed and care for them until they were old enough to leave the nest.

Rosie was impressed by the hummingbirds' dedication to their family. She realized that even though they were small, they were strong and mighty. They worked together to create a home and raise their young, and they never gave up, even when things got tough.

As the days passed, Rosie visited the hummingbirds often, bringing them gifts of nectar and pollen. She watched as the eggs hatched and the babies grew stronger each day. She marveled at how the mother and father worked together to care for

THE LITTLE SNAIL WITH THE BIG HEART: SAMUEL´S ADVENTURES IN THE GARDEN

In a garden filled with blooming flowers, there lived a little snail named Samuel.

Samuel was a small snail with a brown and green shell and a trail of slime behind him wherever he went. Samuel was slow, but he loved exploring the garden and meeting all the other creatures that lived there.

One day, as Samuel was crawling across a leaf, he heard a rustling sound. He looked up and saw a large, fluffy caterpillar crawling towards him. The caterpillar was so big that Samuel had never seen anything like it before.

Samuel was nervous, but he wanted to make friends with the caterpillar. So, he slowly crawled up to the caterpillar and introduced himself. The caterpillar smiled and said hello, and soon they became good friends.

Samuel and the caterpillar spent many happy days together, exploring the garden and enjoying the sunshine. They would crawl through the flowers, stopping to admire their beauty and smell their sweet scent. They would also talk to the other creatures in the garden, like the ladybugs and the butterflies, and make new friends.

One day, as Samuel was crawling along, he noticed that he was leaving behind a trail of slime. He had never thought about it before, but he realized that his trail of slime might be useful for other creatures in the garden.

He decided to ask his friend the caterpillar if he could help with anything using his slime trail. The caterpillar thought for a moment and then said, "You know, I've been having trouble getting around lately. My legs are getting tired, and it's hard to crawl up hills. Maybe your slime trail could help me slide along more easily."

Samuel was excited to help his friend, and he started leaving a thicker trail of slime behind him. The caterpillar was amazed at how much easier it was to move around, and he thanked Samuel for his help.

As the days passed, Samuel continued to use his slime trail to help his friends in the garden. He would leave a trail of slime for the ladybugs to follow, so they could find their way back to their homes. He would also leave a trail for the butterflies, so they could follow it to the flowers and collect nectar.

Samuel was happy to help his friends in any way he could. He realized that even though he was small and slow, he had a unique talent that could be useful to others.

One day, as Samuel was crawling along, he heard a loud noise. He looked up and saw a giant lawnmower heading towards him. He was scared and didn't know what to do.

But then he remembered his slime trail. He started leaving a thick trail of slime behind him, hoping that it would slow down the lawnmower. The lawnmower got closer and closer, but just as it was about to run over Samuel, it hit his slime trail and came to a stop.

Samuel was relieved that he was safe, and he realized that his slime trail had saved his life. He was grateful for his talent and knew that he would continue to use it to help others.

From that day on, Samuel became known as the little snail with the big heart. He continued to explore the garden, making new friends and using his slime trail to help others. He was slow, but he was also kind and brave, and that was what made him special.

The other creatures in the garden looked up to Samuel and admired him for his bravery and kindness. They knew that even though he was small, he had a big heart and a unique talent that could be useful to everyone.

And so, Samuel lived a long and happy life in the garden, surrounded by friends who loved him for who he was. He continued to crawl slowly through the flowers, leaving behind a trail of slime

THE MIGHTY MOOSE MAX: A TALE OF FRIENDSHIP, COURAGE, AND CONSERVATION

In the dense forests of North America, a mighty moose named Max roamed free. Max was a majestic creature, with large antlers and a towering presence. He was a gentle giant who loved to graze on the lush vegetation of the forest and explore the vast wilderness.

One sunny day, Max was grazing near a stream when he heard a soft whimpering sound. He followed the sound and found a small fawn lying on the ground, barely able to move. The fawn was injured, and Max knew that he had to help.

Max gently picked up the fawn with his strong jaws and carried it to a nearby clearing. He knew that the fawn needed

help, and he decided to stay with it until it was better. Max spent his days watching over the fawn, making sure it had food and water, and keeping it safe from predators.

As the days passed, Max and the fawn became close friends. The fawn looked up to Max and admired his strength and kindness. Max loved the fawn like it was his own and promised to protect it from harm.

One day, Max and the fawn were playing in the forest when they heard a loud noise. They looked up and saw a group of hunters heading towards them. Max knew that he had to protect the fawn, and he decided to lead the hunters away from it.

Max ran through the forest, with the hunters chasing him. He zigzagged through the trees, using his powerful legs to outrun them. The hunters were determined, but Max was clever, and he soon lost them in the dense forest.

Max returned to the clearing where the fawn was waiting for him. He was exhausted, but he knew that he had saved the fawn's life. The fawn looked up at Max with gratitude, and Max knew that he had made a true friend.

From that day on, Max and the fawn were

inseparable. They roamed the forest together, exploring every corner and enjoying each other's company. Max taught the fawn how to graze and how to avoid danger, and the fawn learned from Max's wisdom and strength.

One day, Max and the fawn were grazing near a river when they heard a loud noise. They looked up and saw a group of loggers cutting down the trees. Max knew that this was dangerous, and he decided to do something about it.

He ran towards the loggers, using his powerful legs to move quickly. The loggers were surprised to see such a large animal charging towards them, and they stopped cutting the trees.

Max stood in front of the trees, refusing to move. He knew that the forest was home to many animals, and he didn't want them to lose their homes. The loggers tried to move Max, but he was too strong.

Finally, one of the loggers spoke up. "We didn't know that we were hurting the animals. We're sorry. We'll stop cutting down the trees and find a different way to make a living."

Max was pleased to hear this, and he moved aside so that the loggers could leave. He knew that his actions had made a difference and that he had helped to protect the forest and its inhabitants.

Max and the fawn continued to roam the forest, enjoying the beauty of nature and the joy of friendship. Max had become a hero to the animals of the forest, and he knew that he had made a positive impact on the world around him.

And so, Max continued to live a long and happy life, surrounded by friends who loved and admired him. He was a symbol of strength, kindness, and courage, and his legacy lived on long after he was gone.

THE TIMID RABBIT WHO BECAME BRAVE WITH A LITTLE HELP FROM A FRIEND

Once upon a time, in a cozy little burrow near the edge of a vast meadow, there lived a timid little rabbit named Thumper. Thumper was a small and delicate creature, with soft white fur and big, curious eyes. He loved nothing more than hopping around in the sunshine, nibbling on juicy greens, and playing with his fellow rabbits.

Thumper was content with his simple life, but he couldn't help feeling a little envious of the other animals in the meadow. They all seemed so strong and confident, while Thumper felt small and weak in comparison. He longed to be as brave and bold as the foxes and the hawks and the other predators that roamed the meadow.

One day, Thumper was out exploring the meadow when he heard a loud noise. He looked up and saw a hawk circling overhead, scanning the ground for prey. Thumper was terrified, and he froze in place, hoping that the hawk wouldn't notice him.

But the hawk had spotted Thumper, and it

began to swoop down towards him. Thumper knew that he had to act fast if he wanted to survive. He closed his eyes and prayed for a miracle.

Suddenly, he felt a sharp pain in his leg, and he realized that the hawk had caught him in its talons. Thumper tried to struggle free, but the hawk was too strong. He closed his eyes and braced himself for the worst.

Just then, a loud growl echoed across the meadow, and the hawk released Thumper and flew away in terror. Thumper looked up and saw a large, fierce-looking rabbit standing over him. The rabbit was much bigger than Thumper, with sharp claws and a powerful build. Thumper had never seen such a magnificent rabbit before.

The rabbit introduced himself as Buster, and he explained that he was the leader of a group of rabbits who lived in a nearby meadow. Buster had heard Thumper's cries for help and had rushed to his aid, scaring off the hawk with his fierce growl.

Thumper was amazed and grateful, and he thanked Buster for saving his life. From that day on, Thumper and Buster became fast friends. Buster took Thumper under his wing and taught him how to be brave and confident, even in the face of danger.

Buster showed Thumper how to navigate the meadow and avoid predators, how to dig tunnels and burrows for safety, and how to communicate with other rabbits using a complex system of thumps and hops.

Thumper was a quick learner, and he soon became one of the most skilled and daring rabbits in the meadow. He no longer felt small and weak, but instead, he felt strong and confident, like he could face anything that came his way.

One day, a pack of foxes invaded the meadow, looking for a meal. Thumper and Buster led the charge against the foxes, using their sharp claws and quick reflexes to drive them away. Thumper was amazed at how fearless he felt, and he knew that it was all thanks to Buster's guidance and support.

After the foxes had been driven off, Thumper and Buster sat down together and talked about their experiences. Buster explained that courage wasn't just about being strong and fearless, but also about being compassionate and kind. He told Thumper that true bravery meant standing up for what was right, even if it meant facing difficult challenges.

Thumper listened carefully, and he realized

that Buster was right. Being brave wasn't just about being tough and fierce, but also about being kind and compassionate to others.

From that day on, Thumper dedicated himself to being the bravest and kindest rabbit he could be. He helped the other animals in the meadow, standing

LOST AND FOUND: THE ADVENTURE OF ROCKY THE RACCOON.

In the heart of a dense forest, there lived a curious and mischievous raccoon named

Rocky.

Rocky was always getting into trouble,

digging through garbage cans and raiding gardens for the tastiest fruits and vegetables. Despite his antics, Rocky was loved by all the animals in the forest, who admired his cunning and playful nature.

One day, as Rocky was out on his nightly scavenging run, he stumbled upon a strange object. It was a shiny metal box, with a small handle on the side. Rocky couldn't resist the temptation to investigate, and he eagerly pried open the lid.

To his surprise, the box was filled with all sorts of wonderful treats – nuts, berries, and even bits of leftover bread. Rocky's eyes widened with delight, and he eagerly dug in, savoring the delicious flavors.

But as he ate, Rocky began to feel strange. His head started to spin, and his vision grew blurry. Before he knew it, he had collapsed onto the ground, unconscious.

When Rocky woke up, he found himself in a strange and unfamiliar place. He was lying on a cold metal table, with bright lights shining in his eyes. All around him, strange creatures in white coats were bustling back and forth, speaking in hushed tones.

Rocky was terrified, but he tried to stay calm. He knew that he had to escape, and he started looking around for a way out.

As he looked, Rocky noticed that one of the cages nearby was unlocked. He carefully crept over, avoiding the watchful eyes of the scientists, and slipped inside. It was a tight fit, but he managed to curl up in the corner and hide himself away.

For hours, Rocky waited in the cage, listening to the sounds of the lab around him. He could hear the scientists talking

about all sorts of strange things –
experiments, data, and chemicals that he
had never heard of before.

Finally, as the sun began to rise, Rocky saw
his chance. The scientists were all busy with
their work, and he was able to slip out of
the cage and make a run for it.

As he dashed through the hallways of the
lab, Rocky could feel his heart pounding in
his chest. He knew that he was in danger,
but he was determined to escape and get
back to his home in the forest.

Finally, after what seemed like hours, Rocky
burst through a door and found himself
outside. The cool morning air filled his
lungs, and he felt a sense of relief wash
over him.

But his troubles were not over yet. As he
looked around, Rocky realized that he was
lost. He had no idea where he was or how

to get back to his home.

For days, Rocky wandered through the wilderness, searching for some familiar landmark or sign that would lead him back to the forest. He struggled to find food and water, and he grew weaker with each passing day.

But despite his hardships, Rocky refused to give up. He was determined to find his way home, no matter what.

Finally, after what felt like an eternity, Rocky saw a familiar sight. It was a tall oak tree, with a distinctive gnarled branch that he remembered from his adventures in the forest.

With renewed energy, Rocky rushed towards the tree, his heart filled with joy. As he drew closer, he saw a group of animals gathered beneath its branches – his friends from the forest, who had been searching for him all this time.

Rocky let out a joyous cry, and he raced towards his friends, feeling their warm embraces and hearing their reassuring words.

From that day on, Rocky was a changed raccoon. He still loved to get into trouble, but he had learned a valuable lesson about the dangers of wandering too far from home. He cherished his friends and

ABOUT THE AUTHOR

Abby June is a talented author who specializes in writing books for children. With a passion for storytelling and a keen understanding of what captures the imaginations of young readers, she has quickly become a beloved figure in the world of children's literature.

Abby's love of writing began at a young age, as she found solace and inspiration in the stories that she read. As she grew older, she began to craft her own stories, and soon discovered a natural talent for weaving intricate and engaging tales.